HISPANIC LEADERS OF COURAGE

ELLEN OCHOA

EZRA E. KNOPP

Published in 2026 by The Rosen Publishing Group, Inc.
2544 Clinton Street, Buffalo, NY 14224

First Edition

Editor: Theresa Emminizer
Book Design: Michael Flynn

Photo Credits: Cover, pp. 1, 17 https://commons.wikimedia.org/wiki/File:Ellen_Ochoa,_official_portrait.jpg; (series background) Sergei Mishchenko/Shutterstock.com; p. 5 https://commons.wikimedia.org/wiki/File:Ellen_Ochoa.jpg; p. 7 https://commons.wikimedia.org/wiki/File:Sts056-29-019_(8191168358).jpg; p. 9 https://commons.wikimedia.org/wiki/File:S110E5201_-_STS-110_-_Bursch_and_Ochoa_work_at_the_SSRMS_controls_in_Destiny_during_S0_Truss_installation_on_the_ISS_-_DPLA_-_5727db0261b90c9e1a2802087551b87e.jpg; p. 11 https://commons.wikimedia.org/wiki/File:Ellen_Ochoa_(29863224741).jpg; p. 13 https://commons.wikimedia.org/wiki/File:Astronaut_Ellen_Ochoa_(4615699792).jpg; p. 15 https://commons.wikimedia.org/wiki/File:Ellen_Ochoa_carries_her_son_Wilson.jpg; p. 19 https://commons.wikimedia.org/wiki/File:President_Joe_Biden_presents_the_Medal_of_Freedom_to_Ellen_Ochoa.jpg; p. 21 Photo Win1/Shutterstock.com.

Cataloging-in-Publication Data

Names: Knopp, Ezra E.
Title: Ellen Ochoa / Ezra E. Knopp.
Description: Buffalo, NY : PowerKids Press, 2026. | Series: Hispanic leaders of courage | Includes glossary and index.
Identifiers: ISBN 9781499451061 (pbk.) | ISBN 9781499451078 (library bound) | ISBN 9781499451085 (ebook)
Subjects: LCSH: Ochoa, Ellen–Juvenile literature. | Women astronauts–United States–Biography–Juvenile literature. | Astronauts–United States–Biography–Juvenile literature. | Hispanic American astronauts–United States–Biography–Juvenile literature. | Hispanic American women–Biography–Juvenile literature.

Classification: LCC TL789.85.O25 K567 2026 | DDC 629.450092–dc23

Manufactured in China

CPSIA Compliance Information: Batch #QSPK26. For Further Information contact Rosen Publishing at 1-800-237-9932.

CONTENTS

The First Latina in Space

Ellen Ochoa was the first Hispanic woman in space! She worked for NASA for 30 years. During that time, Ellen flew on four space shuttle missions, or trips, logging almost 1,000 hours in space! As a Hispanic leader, Ellen's work has helped make a path for **minorities** and women in science.

BLOOMFIELD FRICK SMITH ROSS
ELLEN OCHOA
NASA

Early Life

Ellen Ochoa was born on May 10, 1958. She was the middle of five children. Ellen's family lived in La Mesa, California. Her grandparents were Mexican **immigrants**. From a young age, Ellen loved math and music. At 10 years old she started playing the flute.

PAYLOAD OPS
A 16

Education

Ellen was the top of her class in high school. She studied **physics** at San Diego State University. Later, she went on to Standford University, where she earned **degrees** in science and electrical engineering. As a **researcher**, Ellen helped come up with important **systems** that made space travel better.

SSC 7

Becoming an Astronaut

In 1990, Ellen was chosen to take part in NASA's astronaut training program. In this program she learned more about science and how to survive, or live, in space. On July 11, 1991, Ellen Ochoa passed training and officially became the first Latina astronaut!

POWER
ON
OFF

Space Missions

In 1993, Ellen took her first trip to space on the shuttle *Discovery*. She also flew on missions in 1994, 1999, and 2002. In space, Ellen researched the sun and Earth's atmosphere. During her 1999 trip, Ellen was part of the crew that first docked, or joined, with the International Space Station.

IMAX

Personal Life

While earning her many **achievements** at work, Ellen Ochoa also made a family. She met Coe Fulmer Miles while working as a researcher and the two married in 1990. During her years as an astronaut Ellen also had two children. She kept playing her flute and even brought it into space!

ELLEN OCHOA

Space Center Director

In 2013, Ellen became the director, or leader, of NASA's Johnson Space Center. She was the first Hispanic and second woman to have the job! Ellen served as director for five years, leading space missions. In 2017, she was inducted, or welcomed, into the U.S. Astronaut Hall of Fame.

After NASA

To celebrate her work, Ellen was given NASA's highest award, the Distinguished Service Medal. After leaving NASA, Ellen became chair, or leader, of the National Science Board. In 2024, she was awarded the Presidential Medal of Freedom by President Joe Biden. She was the second female astronaut to have been given this award.

Legacy

Today, there are schools in California, New Jersey, Oklahoma, Texas, and Washington named after Ellen Ochoa. She's spent many years speaking to students about the importance of going after their dreams. Ochoa's many achievements have changed not only the **future** of space travel, but the future of Hispanic people and girls in science.

Soaring to Great Heights

May 10, 1958

Ellen Ochoa is born.

July 11, 1991

Ochoa becomes the first Latina astronaut.

1993

Ochoa works on Space Shuttle *Discovery.*

1994

She works on Space Shuttle *Atlantis.*

1999

She works on Space Shuttle *Discovery*.

2002

She works on Space Shuttle *Atlantis.*

2013–2018

Ochoa serves as director of NASA's Johnson Space Center.

2024

Ochoa is awarded the Presidential Medal of Freedom.

GLOSSARY

achievement: A result gained by effort.

degree: An official paper given to someone who has completed certain classes at a college or university.

future: Time to come.

immigrant: A person who comes to a country to live there.

minority: A group of people who are different from the larger group in a country or other area in some way, such as race or religion.

physics: The branch of science that deals with matter and energy, as well as how they interact.

researcher: Someone who does research, or careful study to find new knowledge.

system: A set of steps or way of doing something.

FOR MORE INFORMATION

BOOKS

Marino Walters, Jennifer. *Ellen Ochoa: Breaking Barriers in Space*. Egremont, MA: Red Chair Press, 2025.

Romo Edelman, Claudia and Nathalie Alonso. *Ellen Ochoa*. New York, NY: Roaring Brook Press, 2023.

WEBSITES

Ellen Ochoa
ellenochoa.com/biography/
Learn more about Ellen Ochoa's ongoing work on her website.

NASA
www.nasa.gov/people/ellen-ochoa/
Read more about Ellen Ochoa's work during her 30 years at NASA.

INDEX